Barbara Woodhouse

on

HOW TO TRAIN YOUR PUPPY

RINGPRESS

RINGPRESS

Published by Ringpress Books Ltd,
Spirella House, Bridge Road,
Letchworth, Herts, SG6 4ET

Discounts available for bulk orders
Contact the Special Sales Manager at
the above address. Telephone (0462) 674177

First Published 1992

ISBN 0 948955 52 X

Printed and bound in Singapore
by Kyodo Printing Co

CONTENTS

FOREWORD

By Patrick Woodhouse

My mother was born in Ireland in 1910 at a boys' public school where her father was headmaster. Both her family and the boys at the school had a great many different animals and thus she grew up surrounded by them from a very early age. Dogs and other animals became so much a part of her life that it was obvious from the start that she would have animals around her all her life.

One of my earliest recollections of my mother was that she was always with one or other of her two dogs. In the early Fifties she had a Great Dane which responded so perfectly to her training that it won numerous prizes for obedience work. She realised that she really did have a gift for training dogs and she decided that she must use this gift to help others train their dogs.

She started professionally in 1951 with a dog training club meeting on Croxley Green, just a few yards from our house, which was called Campions. She soon had a class of 25-30 dogs and their owners every Sunday and this led to the founding of four other training clubs, in nearby towns, which were always full of dog owners wishing to learn. Her weekends and evenings were thus spent doing the thing she enjoyed most, the training of dogs.

Her own Great Danes, Juno and Junia, were trained to such a high standard that they could work in films and on TV programmes by just being shown the action. Then by simply giving them a command or signal, they would act out the part to perfection. Juno, mother's best known Great Dane, became known as " Take 1 Juno" on the sets of the studios where she worked with famous actors like Sir Alec Guinness, Clark Gable, Roger Moore, Eric Morecambe, and many others. Her Great Danes acted in more than eighty TV and movie productions in their careers, and many of the films were produced by my mother and often directed by her as well.

Her career really started to take off when she was invited to do a TV series about dog training for the BBC and the series was to be called: Training Dogs The Woodhouse Way. This series became such a success that it was repeated three times during its first year and led to two more series and a host of appearances on other programmes in which she was interviewed and in which she demonstrated her methods of dog training to TV stars such as Terry Wogan and Michael Parkinson. In the United States the programmes of her dog training became so popular that they are still being shown to this very day. She became known as the "Dog Lady" and her books became some of the best-sellers ever known in America. In 1980 she won the cherished TV award presented by the Pye Corporation as the Female TV Personality Of The Year and went on to win the title of the World's Best Dog Trainer. Since those hectic days she has travelled the world demonstrating her methods to countless dog owners and visiting numerous countries, including the United States of America, Canada, Australia, New Zealand, Singapore and many parts of Europe, before her death in 1988 following a stroke.

I hope that you, the reader, will get a great deal of help from this book and that it will answer all your questions about the difficulties many people experience when training their puppies. I am sure that the sense of achievement you will experience when you have successfully trained your dog to do even the simplest of exercises will give you a sense of oneness with your dog that cannot be bettered by a relationship with any other animal. May I wish you every success with your training and hope that your dog will become, to quote my mother: "A DOG THAT IS A PLEASURE TO ALL AND A NUISANCE TO NO ONE."

Remember that an appealing little puppy will soon grow up, so choose a breed that suits the size of your home and your lifestyle.

Chapter One

CHOOSING THE RIGHT DOG

I get masses of letters from people who wish me to choose the breed or sort of dog they should have. They usually write me reams about what they don't want, instead of writing fully to me about their homes, their children, their relatives, their other animals, the amount of time they can give to their dog, etc. They may say that they have heard all long-eared dogs get canker, that all Dachshunds get follicular mange, and class all dogs of those and other particular breeds under one heading as impossible. Dogs are no different to human beings in the wide range of characteristics and temperaments they possess. Dogs can have nervous breakdowns the same as human beings, but dogs get typed as bad-tempered or disobedient. Few people think of the stresses of modern life, the noise of the traffic, the perpetual human rat race which spills off on to the dog as his owner is forever dashing out of the front door leaving the dog behind, bewildered. The slower ordered life of the past has almost disappeared for dogs and owners, and dogs get put to sleep for things which

could be easily cured, if only the owners would understand them and give them time.

The first thing to understand about dogs is that any change of home is traumatic. I was watching a TV programme on disturbed children, and the only thing that had apparently made these children disturbed was that their parents had split up and the children had been put in care. Has it ever struck a new dog owner that exactly this has happened to a dog and that he takes time to readjust himself to a new home, new rules, new food, a new house, new people? Seldom is this given much thought. The new owners conclude that they are acceptable to a dog, in spite of the fact that to a dog they may not have the right scent. They may not handle him correctly; the voice may grate; they may have someone in the house who hates dogs; they may have an enemy cat which would willingly scratch out the new dog's eyes if he wasn't careful to avoid it. People should understand life from a dog's point of view before blaming everything that goes wrong on the dog. Mothers-to-be buy every book

Think about how much care the dog's coat will need when it is an adult.

they can on baby welfare, but hundreds of people buy dogs with very little knowledge of them and then blame the dog for his behaviour. I would suggest that before anyone gets a dog, they should examine their knowledge of the breed they are choosing. Talk to people who have owned these dogs, see them at a dog show. If the breed shows aggression towards other dogs in the ring, or extreme nerves when handled by the judge, think twice before buying one. Temperament faults are the most difficult to cure, and it may cost a lot to have professional help in this matter.

The most important thing to arrange before a puppy joins the household is to think how he is going to fit in the daily life and routine of the home. So many people just buy a puppy on impulse, never realising that a young puppy is just as much trouble to begin with as a young baby, if you wish to train him quickly to be a trouble-free occupant of the home. People forget that if you want, for example, to house train a puppy quickly you cannot, at first, go out all evening to dinner and a theatre. For the hours you would be away would mean that you could not take the puppy out often enough to make him clean. When I had a new puppy recently I gave up six weeks of my life to his early training and I reckoned that the time was well spent. Few people, I think, would take their duty to their puppy as seriously as that. From the very beginning it must be decided which member of the household is going to look after the puppy, and as far as possible, the routine should be stuck to. Puppies get 'set in their ways' and a strict routine is essential for health and training. Think about how much

exercise you are going to be able to give your dog; if it is somewhat restricted either due to your age, your work, or your health, don't go and buy a Great Dane or a Dobermann. Think about the dog's coat; have you time to brush him as often as he needs doing? There is nothing more horrible than an Old English Sheepdog or a Bearded Collie that is all matted.

Make up your mind what role the dog has to play in your home. Is he just a pet? If so, you can often buy a puppy not up to show standard cheaper from a breeder, than one with show potential. But don't rave if you take him to the local show and find he has an undershot jaw or some other fault, for you must have known he had some fault to get him cheaper. Don't take it out on the dog, for dogs understand your moods and your thoughts, and if you are thinking unpleasant thoughts about your dog, he will pick it up and be down-hearted. In the matter of intelligence, dogs like humans, vary enormously. The development of the brain is, to a certain extent, hereditary. The puppy must have an aptitude for the work he is expected to carry out. For example, Pekingeses would not make good gundogs, their physical form does not lend itself to the work. Some breeds, undoubtedly, through generations of training for work, have developed better brains a quick alertness which makes training their brains easy. On the other hand, Dalmatians are not so easily educated.

If the aptitude is there, it is up to the owners to encourage the dog to use his brains, and if training goes steadily along set lines, this development of brain power is quite remarkable. Few

Some breeds like Collies are easy to train.

owners really get the best out of their dogs: they should start developing the puppy's aptitude for work at a very early age. In fact, I think eight weeks old is the time to begin in a small way. The puppy should be talked to in a sensible way; made to do things for you like carrying things; taught words like 'Here's Master, go and see him'; 'Who's that?', and other sentences which are relevant to everyday life in the home. I think the aptitude of the owner for training the puppy is more essential than the aptitude of the puppy to absorb the training.

Before buying a dog you should decide whether you would be better suited to a male or a female. This is largely a matter of personal choice, but there are other pros and cons which

should be weighed up. Bitches come into season, and this has to be coped with, making sure that no unwanted matings take place. Most bitches come on heat for the first time at about eight to ten months, but some don't come on until twelve months. There is no fixed time, so don't worry if your puppy is late. The season lasts from seventeen to twenty-one days. If it doesn't go after twenty-one days, consult your vet. The bitch is ready from the mating point of view from about the eighth to the fifteenth day. Before that dogs will not pay much attention to her. Some bitches are highly irregular, so it is never safe to go by this. Amplex pills given every twenty-four hours do much to protect your bitch from the unwelcome attention of dogs. The ordinary Amplex should be given by day. Four pills every four hours, and two 'Clinical' Amplex at night. These clinical ones are double strength and last until you can give the ordinary ones in the morning again. It doesn't matter how much you give a bitch, they are harmless. You can increase the dosage if dogs still pay her unwelcome attention.

Male dogs do not have the problem of coming into season, but some owners find that a male tends to have more of a wander lust than a bitch, for obvious reasons, and they can be more aggressive with other dogs. However, the fundamental issue is to teach your dog to respect you, so that he is always under your control, and he does not just take off when it suits him. I have also had letters complaining of male dogs being 'over-sexed', and a nuisance to every dog they come across. In my opinion, castration is the best way to deal with an over-sexed puppy. He will not get better as he grows older, as some people would have you believe. The tearing up of bedding is all part of the sex urge, and eventually he will mount people's legs, to the intense embarrassment of all those concerned. Castration, if done young, has no bad effect on the puppy at all, and the result will be fairly speedy. If left until the dog is really a confirmed nuisance, the time it takes to have effect is much longer. Most vets do the operation overnight and let the puppy go home the next morning. There need be no stitches in the incision. After a week the puppy is quite over it. Some vets put in stitches, but these do occasionally get infected. So keep an eye on the puppy's backside for at least a week to see all is healing well. A castrated puppy should be strictly dieted to keep his figure. He is inclined to beg for food. There are no harmful effects after castration. I think all male dogs, kept as pets only, would benefit by this operation. They are much nicer to own, and remain gay and happy.

If you decide to go ahead and buy a dog, a holiday abroad is out of the question owing to quarantine regulations. To most of us dog lovers these restrictions are taken as a matter of course. The dog is part of the family, and we wouldn't leave one of the family behind. Some owners are lucky enough to know that their dogs will be happy if provided with good boarding conditions in well-run kennels, and this holiday problem does not exist for them. What does exist for all owners is the risk of the dog getting ill and needing very special care; often the disease produces horrible symptoms and one has to carry out duties which are repulsive; before having a dog you must decide that you are willing to undertake his care 'in sickness and in health'. Are you willing to prepare his food and see that he gets the right diet, or is he just going to live on anything that comes his way? Most dogs thrive best on regular meals, at regular times, of the correct food in the correct proportions. Sometimes it is a nuisance to have to go and buy the dog's food when you are busy, or have to cook it. Think of this before you become a dog owner.

When you have taken all these points into consideration, ensuring that you really do want a dog and are prepared to care for it properly, then, and only then are you ready to think about the breed of dog that you want. I think dog owners can be rash in the breed of dog

Dalmatians are harder to train, but patience and perseverance will win the day.

they choose. I wish they would find out more about what the dogs were originally bred for, before they buy one. All the bull-breeds were bred for fighting in one way or another, also the Irish terriers and Kerry Blues. Why do weak little owners want this type of dog? Is it that they lack courage in their make-up and buy a courageous dog to compensate? If you are a flat dweller choose a dog that needs little exercise or work like the King Charles Spaniel, whose ancestors are so often pictured in old oil paintings and whose lives in various courts of royalty were well known. I have met a family who expected a Beagle to lead this sort of life and who complained when it became unmanageable. One Beagle in a family of children must be a misfit. They are hunting dogs, not playthings, and they have very stubborn natures. The choice of dog must of course rest with the buyer, but I do feel breeders could refuse to sell an old lady a Bloodhound, or a small child a big boisterous breed. I suppose those who breed dogs do so for profit, and few can afford to refuse a sale. I only wish they had the dogs to deal with when they become problem dogs, and it would then deter them from selling unsuitable dogs.

The best age to buy a puppy is when it fully weaned, at six weeks.

Chapter Two

ARRIVING HOME

The best age to buy a puppy is when he has been safely weaned and is no longer in need of the warmth of his brothers and sisters. This is approximately at six weeks. Many people buy them younger; in fact I have seen people buy one that I am sure was no older than one month, but the rearing of such a puppy is a hazardous one. Much depends on the size of the puppy you choose. If you are determined to buy the 'runt' of the litter, then it may be wise to wait a week longer before having him than if you were buying the 'pick of the litter'. Dogs very often develop earlier than bitches, but don't be deceived by their little extra size; they are not always the strongest. Puppies should be completely weaned from the mother by six weeks. If you have a warm place for him, sensible ideas about his feeding and rest, do not allow young children to maul him, and do not expect too rapid house-training (for puppies of that age have no control over their bladders or bowels at all), then by all means buy one of six weeks. Many breeders, not wishing for unpleasantness if anything goes wrong, will not part with puppies of this age.

It is quite impossible to sum up at six weeks old what puppies are going to look like at four months. Their eyes are all the same dark blue, then in two months' time they may be a pale yellow, which is most unattractive in most dogs. So if you mind this sort of thing don't buy one too young. Colour changes must be reckoned on as well, for at six weeks the puppy only has his baby coat, and this will not be shed for some time. When his permanent coat does come through, the colour and texture will be somewhat different, but brindles don't become fawns or vice versa, because colour is hereditary, and one can roughly know before buying a puppy what it is likely to look like when adult. When you are ready to collect your puppy you must find out from the person he is coming from exactly what he has been fed on, and at what meal times he has each kind of food. Some diet charts that are sent out by breeders look unnecessarily complicated and expensive, and one often wonders whether the puppy really has had such food. But it is very unwise to change the feeding of a young puppy, so whatever you think, do go by the chart for at least a week, and then, if you wish, modify it in slow stages.

You must have decided before buying the puppy exactly where you intend keeping him. It is not enough to say that the kitchen, for example, will do, you must also have made preparations to house the pup so that he can be kept very warm at first. A basket for a young puppy is not a good idea. Puppies need rest. If a pup is allowed to follow his owners about in the house he will get over-tired. The best solution is to have an indoor kennel. This need not be an elaborate affair, but it should be made large enough to allow the puppy to grow and still use as his resting place when he grows old enough to be free in the house. There is nothing so useful as to have somewhere you can put the dog, knowing he cannot get into mischief when you are out or busy for a few hours. When the dog is about six months old he can have a basket, but personally I don't like round ones. The dog's natural sleeping position, when really sound asleep, is on his side with his legs stretched out. Unless the basket is much too big, this attitude cannot be achieved. Therefore I think an oblong bed which is on legs, is a much better form of sleeping arrangement for the dog. Best of all I like an old chair. These can be bought cheaply at any furniture sale; and have the advantage of being off the floor with side protection to keep the puppy free from draughts. The puppy must be taught from an early age to go to his bed and stay there when told. If visitors come to the house the puppy is then not a nuisance to them.

Care must be taken if the puppy is coming to a home where there are children. The best thing to do with very young children and a new puppy is to supervise their play. When the puppy shows signs of being tired, and of being mauled about, take him away and put him in his indoor kennel to sleep. Remember small puppies need an awful lot of sleep. At six weeks they should not be out of their sleeping quarters for more than three hours a day, and that should be in small bouts at a time. The child should never be allowed to go and interfere with a resting puppy, or indeed, a resting adult. The dog's kennel or basket should be private, so that he can feel that when he is there, he is free from being interfered with or annoyed.

Children don't mean to annoy a puppy, but they like carrying the pup about, which few puppies like, and children draw their hands up to escape the nips, and that makes the puppy jump up, as he may think they are playing. The puppy then gets smacked for jumping up and he doesn't know where he is. Any child over about six years old should be able to be very useful in the training of a puppy. If you eventually take your puppy to training classes, try to take the child along too. My own little girl, when she was six years old, trained her four-months-old black-and-tan terrier with very little help from me. It was lovely to watch the two of them performing in competitive obedience against German Shepherds and other larger dogs. By all means let the child help to feed the puppy. If the pup does not pull on the lead, let the child hold it when you are out walking in a safe district. Never, however, let a child hold the lead when the puppy is in the town. The pup might suddenly get a fright from a bang, or from being attacked by another dog and might snatch his lead free. If the puppy got run over as a result, the child would never get over it. Not only that, unless the child keeps the puppy properly under control, the pair can be a nuisance to others in crowded streets. Remember, everyone does not like children or dogs.

The puppy should be firmly scolded by the parents of the child if the pup does lose his temper and attempt to bite the child. A dog won't grow out of these things; he will grow worse if not corrected whilst still young. The puppy should have bones given to him, and they should be taken away with the command "Give", and then given back again. If the puppy shows signs of growling or biting when this is done, he must be scolded in a very cross voice. But remember that the child must not be allowed to tease the puppy by taking the bone away every time the puppy is enjoying it. When you really wish to take the bone away, do so quickly and firmly. Get the puppy accustomed to having his mouth opened when he picks up something you don't wish him to have. This opening of the mouth will help in later life if you need to give medicine.

A puppy can get into a habit of growling when the owner tries to pick him up or to take away something he is playing with. Novice owners think the best remedy is to smack the puppy on the nose, but I think this is a cruel and ineffective practice. If you ever have to smack a puppy do it with the palm of your hand over his hindquarters. I find, however, that a good shake and a thunderous voice are far more effective.

If a puppy persists in growling, you must make him understand immediately that he must do as you ask. The best way to do this is to keep a choke chain on the puppy, and when you want something and the puppy growls, just suspend him until he gasps for breath, when the object you want will fall from his mouth. Immediately praise the puppy – a tremendous show of affection is absolutely necessary.

Growling, curiously enough, is not always a sign of bad temper, sometimes it is purely and simply 'talking'. My own Dane puppy often growls when her tail is wagging furiously, and I am scratching her chest. It is a sort of series of grunts of happiness. To anyone who didn't know her, she would appear to be growling menacingly. A puppy often growls because it is over-tired and wants to be left alone. All puppies should have ample rest. Any sign of growling should be a warning to the owner to put the puppy into its indoor kennel or basket and let it sleep. After all, what other sign can a puppy give to show that it has had enough of something?

A number of people who go out and buy a puppy already have another pet, such as a cat, at home, and they are worried about how to introduce the two so that they learn to live together amicably. This is a very knotty problem, and one that often has no solution. If your cat has been friendly with a previous dog there should not be much to worry about. Just keep the puppy from annoying the cat for about a week, but if the cat has never seen a dog before, it will take much longer. I personally take the cat and dog on to my lap and stroke them both hard, not allowing the cat to run away. The other

Take care when you introduce a puppy to a home where there are children and other pets.

method I have used is to make a double cage divided by strong wire-netting and make them sleep side by side. After this there is seldom any more trouble. Some cats however, are born nasty with dogs, and it will not be safe for any puppy to be with that type of cat, for it will surely scratch the puppy's eyes.

Never encourage any puppy to chase cats, it is cruel and quite useless, for the dog will never catch the cat, even if that is why you teach the puppy to be so horrid. Should your puppy show any signs of cat-chasing put him on a long cord if a cat is likely to be around, and when he starts to go after the cat jerk really hard on the check cord, and give the puppy a tremendous scolding with the word "leave". Cat chasing may easily lead to chicken chasing or even sheep killing. It is up to you to check this tendency from the start of it. A small kitten and a puppy are ideal friends, and there is no better way to teach friendliness than to have one of each. Don't be worried if the bigger puppy occasionally carries the cat around by the neck. This frequently happens and is only a sign of good friendship.

Puppies can be very destructive in a garden, and if you are a keen gardener and you want your garden to remain unspoilt there are certain steps you should take. There is only one way to teach your puppy to keep off the garden, and that is to put wire netting temporarily round the flower beds and valuable shrubs. Pampas grass has a fatal fascination for puppies and they can completely wreck it in a few minutes of play. The words "No, naughty!" must be used in a thunderous tone if the puppy attempts to go on the flower beds. Teach him basic obedience, and never leave him free and alone in the garden before he is properly trained. That is the golden rule when owning a puppy and a garden. Make sure the puppy never empties its bladder on your lawn. The urine of a bitch is fatal to lawns. It first look as if the urine has killed the grass on the lawn, and then the grass grows dark green and coarse, which is most unsightly. Keep a rough patch of grass for the puppy's toilet and make him always use it.

Chapter Three

HOUSE TRAINING

This is an extremely difficult subject to tackle, as I don't know in what circumstances many dogs have to be trained. But as far as general principles go, I think all dogs must be treated in the same way. First, the owner of a new puppy must realise that this puppy has been brought up in a kennel or shed where he has been able to run about and relieve himself at any time, day or night, and it is a great change for him to have to learn to do otherwise. But what does help is that in his new home he is fed at regular intervals, and can't just go and have a drink from his mother at any time. As it is a natural reflex for the puppy to wish to pass water after a feed, this is the first clue to a method of house-training. Always put your puppy out immediately after a meal, and give him the command you will use for ever after. I use the words "Hurry up" because no one else knows what I am talking about; but it doesn't matter which words you use, so long as in the future your puppy is going to connect those words with his obligations. Immediately the puppy has obeyed your wishes, praise him for all you are worth,

then take him in and have a game. Soon after a short gambol, he will feel tired and comfortable after his meal, and he may then safely be put in his basket or kennel, or whatever you are going to keep him in in the house.

I strongly recommend all puppy owners to buy an indoor kennel such as a welded wire folding indoor kennel. The use of the indoor kennel is very important, and the first step is to consider where to site it. I strongly recommend the kitchen, as it will be both warm and have a floor which will not be damaged in the event of an accident. I would then put a nice, warm blanket or cushion in the bedroom end of the kennel and adapt the far end for house-training purposes. To do this, cover the sheet metal floor with a piece of real or plastic turf. The puppy then has an area to do his 'jobs' if he feels desperate and cannot wait for his master to take him out. The turf should be changed – or washed if it is plastic – every two days.

The next question in house training arises when your puppy wakes up after a long sleep; you must then be ready to

A folding indoor kennel is ideal for puppy owners.

rush him out of doors. Most puppies will whimper when they wake up, to show that they are ready for a playtime or a meal. (It is absolutely vital that a young puppy should be kept warm if you want him to become clean quickly; a cold puppy cannot control his bladder.) Next comes the vexed question as to what one should do when a puppy makes a puddle on the floor. Some people advise rubbing his nose in it. What a wicked idea! Should the puppy make a puddle, catch him, show him what he has done, and scold him resoundingly by your tone of voice, then immediately take him out to his usual spot. This usual spot is another vital chain in the training link. The puppy quickly gets to connect that spot with his 'jobs' and associations are quickly made. If, after puddling the floor, you put him out and he does it again outside, praise him

fervently, and with great love in your voice.

The most difficult thing to do is to train your dog to be clean the night through, and I sometimes have had my puppy to sleep in my room so that immediately he wakes I rush downstairs with him, and out. I know it's as bad as having to attend to a baby, but I have always had my tiny puppies clean at about nine weeks; in fact, I have twice had six-week-old puppies quite safe to take into hotels with me, with never a mistake. But to achieve this one must always be watching the puppy, and at the slightest sign of sniffling around in an interested manner, one must whip the puppy up in one's arms and put him out. Fear can often be a cause of puppies failing to be clean. Dogs wet the carpets, just as children wet their beds, normal house training breaks

Place a piece of real or plastic turf at one end of the kennel for emergencies.

down and desperate owners write to me for new training methods. All that is wanted to right the trouble is to give the dog confidence. Put him in the kitchen where the floor can be washed, praise the dog when you greet him in the morning, completely ignoring the puddle, give only one meal early in the day and restrict drinking after 5pm, and in most cases the trouble clears up. The poor dog knows he has done wrong to puddle, even the tiniest puppy learns quickly what is right or wrong. Add to the dog's fear when he has made a mistake and you will never cure the fault. I have known a night or two with

the owner in their bedroom to cure this fault completely, for the dog rests peacefully.

Dogs undoubtedly suffer night terrors if they are highly-strung, and develop all sorts of queer faults, yet these faults have been found to disappear on holiday when the dog has been with you day and night. I always believe dogs are like small children, and well I remember lying awake as a small child on Nanny's day out suffering tortures for fear she might get run over by a bus, and not until she came home did I fall asleep. I think the same thing happens with beloved highly-strung dogs: the night is long for them, where they cannot hear their owner, and they sleep restlessly and then their bladder plays them up and a puddle results. Think before you punish a dog that has been perfectly clean in the past.

I believe the owner's voice is the thing that makes many dogs delinquent. The hopelessly inadequate tone of voice on giving a command. The lack of meaningful words, the dreadfully flat tone they use for praise and the laziness of their movement all go to make a dog bored and uncaring. For example, if the owner sees a puppy just about to soil the floor or actually in the act, she should leap to scold it and pick it up and put it out. That leap instils into the dog's mind that there is something wrong with what he was doing or was about to do. A loud "Naughty dog" completes the correction. Never rub a dog's nose in what it has done – that is useless and not understood by a dog, and it is unhygienic and unkind.

We now come to the problem of flat-dwellers, probably unable to get up and down stairs quickly enough; the best thing for them to do is to have a large tray or flat box in one corner of the room or landing, filled with earth or whatever you wish to use, and to get the puppy used to going on to that. But, of course, that does not implant the idea in the puppy's mind that it is wrong to soil in a house. I really feel that if flat dwellers must have a young puppy, they should make the effort to take him out into the street. Should a puppy ever be smacked for being dirty? I think he should after the age of six months, providing he has been given every chance to be clean. I have known puppies go out and have a good time

and immediately come in and disgrace themselves in the house. That is the time to pick the puppy up and show him what you are smacking him for; give him two or three sound smacks on his rump and put him out again.

Now comes the question of how to keep a puppy warm at night so that he sleeps right through and therefore doesn't wet his box. I always recommend putting puppies in their indoor kennel in the hot cupboard at nights with the door ajar for air. Put a very warm cushion in the box so that when the puppy is lying down the pillow billows up round him much as a litter of other puppies would. A hot-water bottle is not a good idea. These get cold too soon, and there is always the risk of the bottle getting chewed and the contents soaking the box. If you put the puppy's box by a fire it gets cold towards morning, and a cold puppy is inevitably a dirty, wet puppy.

The other thing that helps a puppy to become clean quickly is to give him his milk or liquid feeds early in the day. Keep the meat or solid feed for the evening meal. I always give the last meal at ten o'clock at night, as dogs have very slow digestions and that meal lasts well round until the morning. I give the last sloppy meal at four o'clock. Be sure to take the puppy out to his favourite spot last thing before you go to bed. We have a tiny black and tan miniature terrier which we took on a tour, staying at different hotels each night, and we never had any mistakes with her. We had her blanket and wrapped her up in it at night and put her with the door very slightly ajar in the cupboard usually kept by the bed. It made a snug bed, and I could hear her immediately she

A cold puppy is inevitably a dirty, wet puppy.

woke. If there was a balcony I popped her out on that; if not I went downstairs to the garden. For all these reasons, it is always best to buy a puppy in the summer months: I have never had to house-train one in this way in mid-winter.

The best chance of getting a clean puppy within reasonable time is never to allow him to be free in any room, when very tiny, unless you are there to watch him. Pop him back in his kennel when you have to go out of the room. It teaches him to lie quietly in the one place, and he comes to look upon it as his very own home. A dirty dog in the house is usually a consequence of the owner's just not taking enough trouble to watch the puppy and rush him out quickly. Mothers of children know how essential this watching is; so should dog owners. If a reasonably adult dog continues to have dirty habits, restrict his fluid intake after 4pm, and, of course, confine him in an indoor kennel. People often go on far too long giving their puppies milk. I think after six months old this is unnecessary and adds to the fluid intake because the puppy likes it, then he has to pass more urine. With correct feeding and adequate supplement of minerals and trace elements, the dog should not need milk.

Much the most difficult trouble to overcome is the reluctance of a bitch to relieve herself except in her accustomed spot at home. I have never known a dog suffer from this particular inhibition, so different is his nature. I have known bitches hold out for well over twelve hours, and it is extremely bad for them. This is where training helps, for if you always use one unvarying word, and expect the bitch to relieve herself when you employ it, she will then know it is not wrong to use a different place. It is usually most difficult when you have a bitch used to using only grass – that is why I advocate also teaching her to go on a concrete surface. It is all association of words and deed, and this association must be established at a very early age if you are to avoid snags like this. Other considerations apart, it is extremely annoying to have to walk your bitch for a long time, say in rainy or bitter weather, when, had she been taught to behave on command, time and temper could have been saved and the risk of catching cold obviated. I have never known this inhibition occur in kennel dogs, it is usually confined to very clean, house-trained animals.

Good feeding is the key to a happy, healthy dog.

Chapter Four

FEEDING

The feeding regime you adopt for your puppy will depend on his age, and it is the number of feeds per day that is as important as the quantity of food that is offered. All puppies of six weeks need five meals a day. I think 6.30am, 10.30am, 2 30pm and 6.30pm should be the main meals, and then last thing at night give a warm drink of milk. Should a puppy be noisy at night it often pays to give one of the heavy meals at night which includes meat, cereal and milk. No puppy should run about after a meal. He should rest after having been taken out for toilet purposes. It is most important to see that the puppy digests his meals in peace. Don't allow children to interfere with him or play with him for at least an hour. Always remember a puppy will eat until he is nearly ready to burst. Never increase the food beyond the correct amount in the mistaken idea that he is still a hungry 'poor little thing'. If you over-feed a puppy the food will only pass out of the body as urine or faeces. His body cannot absorb more than a certain amount. Excess food gives rise to flatulence and distension, both of which are uncomfortable for the puppy and unpleasant for the people he lives with. Distension can be dangerous and can actually kill a puppy.

No puppy can grow bigger than he is genetically designed to be; more food won't make him grow any bigger. Too little food, on the other hand, can stunt him. Regularity of meals is of the utmost importance, because the puppy's saliva begins to flow at that time. In this saliva are the enzymes, etc., which help to break down the proteins and fats in the body. Even rattling his feeding bowl will make a puppy's saliva flow. Association of ideas is of paramount importance in the dog world. So if you are an unpunctual person, you must change now where your puppy is concerned. No puppy should be fed at the mealtimes of his owner, or he may start begging at meals. There is nothing so annoying as having a dog watch every mouthful that goes in your own mouth. He sits there with a dejected expression and one feels a brute if one doesn't share the meal with him. The result of sharing a meal is that the puppy's tummy gets upset, for it never knows when to expect food. The puppy probably gets too fat with having more than its rightful diet, and altogether it is a bad thing for both puppy and owner.

The meals should roughly consist of two-thirds protein and one-third carbohydrates in the form of meat and bread or biscuits. Milk should always be given, and added minerals and vitamins are of vital importance to make growth and impart good health to the puppy. There are three main ways of feeding puppies. I shall give you two or three guidelines. You must use your commonsense as to quantities, and vary them to suit your particular puppy.

There are three main ways of bringing up a puppy. The first is on an ordinary household diet of warm cow's milk, scraped beef and brown bread, coupled with an occasional egg and vitamins such as A and D in the form of cod-liver oil or capsules. The second is on the diet provided by the manufacturers of dog food, and this now comes in two forms. It can consist of tinned meat and puppy meal, changing to biscuits as the puppy grows older, with the addition of cow's milk. Or you can feed a complete dried food, and these are usually designed for puppies, with a different type for adult dogs. It is always important to follow the manufacturer's instructions on complete diets, and ensure that sufficient quantities of liquid are offered. The third diet you can feed is a a natural diet consisting of raw beef, wholemeal biscuits, and carrot and grass meal with the addition of seaweed and natural

minerals etc. Although these diets may appear very different, they are all offering basically the same: supplying milk, cereals and meat. Some people try to rear their dogs on a vegetarian diet, but dogs' digestions are made to deal with meat; they are carnivorous animals, not herbivorous ones, therefore these diets must be unsuitable for puppies.

The quantities given in the following diets are for puppies of eight to ten weeks, weighing when adult about 25lbs. Larger or smaller breeds must have larger or smaller amounts in proportion. Appetite is the greatest guide to feeding. If anything is left on the puppy's dish after a meal, it is being over-fed and should have the next meal reduced accordingly. A puppy should always be willing to eat more after its meal, but should not be given more than the right amount. The right amount of daily intake is about half an ounce per pound of body weight. This must of necessity, be a rough guide. The larger breeds like Great Danes could not be fed this way as their rate of growth is so quick.

Most people start their puppies off with a milky porridge for breakfast. I then provide three meat meals and offer milk as a drink with each of these. The meat should be scraped beef, unless a proprietary brand of meat is used. Mutton, veal and pork are not so good. A puppy's digestion is judged by his bright eye, his normally formed stools, his clean-smelling breath and his gaiety. A dull, listless puppy is a wrongly-fed or an ill puppy. The eating of earth or stones is due to either a mineral deficiency or worms. Correctly fed puppies do not eat earth or manure.

HOUSEHOLD DIET

6.30am: Warm milk and about a dessertspoonful to a tablespoonful of porridge or cereal according to age and size.
10.30am: 2oz scraped beef, drink of milk.
2.30pm: Brown bread and milk.
6pm: Scraped beef and cornflakes or bread, drink of milk.
10pm: Drink of milk.

As the puppy gets bigger he will drop the porridge feed, and one more meal of scraped beef will be added. At twelve weeks the meals will be reduced to four a day, then three and, lastly, at six months old they will be reduced to two. By this age a puppy of Spaniel size would be having half a pound of raw beef per day, plus four slices of brown bread or two cupfuls of biscuit meal, soaked in boiling water or gravy and allowed to cool before feeding, and a drink of milk. In comparison, a Great Dane at six months old would be having one pound of meat per day, one pint of milk, six slices of brown bread, biscuits or cornflakes. A Dane never needs more than one and a half pounds of meat per day, and bread or biscuits are given according to appetite and condition. All puppies need the addition of vitamins and minerals to their diet to assist teething and growth.

If a puppy scratches, the diet should be changed as he is possibly allergic to something in the diet, or is being overfed. A bad-tempered puppy is usually one that has indigestion – mostly due to overfeeding. Titbits are enjoyed by puppies, but are not good for them in any quantity. The puppy's saliva runs at meal times, so punctuality is of paramount importance. If you are travelling with a puppy it is better to take tinned meat than fresh meat. Any plain human biscuits can be substituted when travelling, for bread or dog biscuits. Milk should be taken in a bottle and if necessary boiled before the journey to stop it going sour. Goat's milk can be fed to puppies, but it has a higher fat content than cow's milk and therefore may not be so well tolerated.

GENERAL GUIDE FOR FEEDING MEDIUM-SIZED DOGS WEIGHING FROM 20-30LB WHEN ADULT
(Smaller or larger breeds in proportion)

EIGHT TO TWELVE WEEKS

7.30am: Drink of warm cow's milk.
9.30am: 1 1/2 oz of fresh or tinned meat and half a teacupful of puppy meal or two slices of brown bread, soaked in meat stock.
3pm: Drink of milk with brown bread or a puppy biscuit.
6pm: 1 1/2 oz minced beef cooked or raw or tinned meat with cornflakes or half a cupful of soaked puppy meal.
10.pm: Drink of warm milk.

TWELVE WEEKS TO SIX MONTHS

7.30am: Drink of cow's milk, two toasted slices of brown bread with butter or a few ovals of puppy meal.
12 noon: 2-4 oz tinned meat or minced cooked beef or fish (Coley).
6pm: 2-4 oz fresh or tinned meat mixed with dry brown bread on half a cup of puppy meal soaked beforehand. A drink of milk.

SIX MONTHS ONWARDS

As a dog reaches six months and over, the feeds are gradually reduced to two a day, 1/2lb of beef or one small tin of dog meat and about a teacupful of biscuit meal and a drink of milk should keep a dog healthy, providing vitamins are added to the diet in some form.

Fatness only comes from over-feeding. This is extremely bad for any puppy. If you are the sort of owner who over-feeds, anyway, either because you don't know what diet to give or because you give in to every demand from the puppy for food, you are not likely to get your puppy's 'vital statistics' right again very easily. Labradors, for example, should have about 1lb of meat and 1/2lb of biscuits a day when seven to eight months old, plus half a pint of milk. If the puppy still stays fat on this, cut his biscuits. Dogs can live and be very healthy entirely fed on the protein diet of meat. It is only the fat and carbohydrates which cause a puppy to get fat. Obesity is bad for the heart, puts a strain on the kidneys, and makes the puppy out of breath. Fat puppies usually suffer from 'wind' and occasionally have unpleasant breath. They don't live as long as properly dieted dogs. There is only one advantage in having a fairly plump puppy. If he does get ill he has plenty of weight to lose.   A puppy's appetite should always be a keen one. The puppy who doesn't bolt his food is not completely healthy. You are either over-feeding him or wrongly feeding him. A lot of people over-feed their puppies just because they appear hungry. If, however, the appetite is poor, cut the quantity of food until the appetite returns, having made sure the puppy is well. Frequent small feeds are better than less frequent large ones. Fat is a thing small puppies seem unable to digest in great quantities, and this often makes a puppy have a poor appetite. Cut out eggs, take the cream off the milk and give lean scraped beef and the puppy's appetite should then return. The puppy should lick his dish feverishly when he has had his meal; that shows he would eat more and his appetite is good. Don't be tempted to give him more than the right amount or his digestion will suffer. A puppy's tummy is very tiny, and if you distend it with too big a meal he will get flatulence, and with a big breed it may make the puppy's front legs bow if he gets too heavy from over-feeding. A puppy should always be ready for its meals. If he is not, don't leave the food about; take it away and throw it away, for the food should always be completely fresh. If the puppy doesn't want his food for more than one meal, consult your vet. t

There can be no hard and fast rule about the quantity of water a puppy should drink. You should always leave clean water in a place he knows so that he can help himself. If he is thirsty he will drink water – if he is not thirsty he will be satisfied with his drinks of milk. Any excess fluid is passed off by the kidneys. It is far more dangerous for a puppy to drink too little than too much. All animals thrive much better with water ad lib. Drinking water should be at roughly room temperature. I always place the drinking trough on a baking tin, as most puppies are rather sloppy drinkers and splash the carpet. If a puppy is ill, he can live only on clean drinking water for quite a time; never force food down him.

Chapter Five

CARING FOR YOUR PUPPY

INOCULATIONS

There are always people ready to tell you of the awful things that happen in life whatever you do. The risk of anything happening to your puppy after being inoculated is so small that I personally would never think about it. Some inoculations have dead germs in them, some have modified live ones that have been rendered just strong enough to do their job, which is to give the animal enough of them to encourage the body to make enough antibodies to set up a future resistance to that disease. In humans smallpox vaccination is one of this type, that is why babies that are inoculated get a reaction; yet few sensible mothers would deny their babies this safeguard against such a horrible disease if their child risked catching it. You should look at inoculations against the major diseases in the same light. Millions of dogs are protected by these inoculations and slowly these terrible diseases are being wiped out. All vets have their own policies on vaccination programmes, but the majority will inoculate against distemper, leptospirosis, hepatitis and parvovirus.

There are, however, one or two things you ought to do when your dog is inoculated, and the first is to make sure your vet does not give the injection in the shoulder. This has been known to make the dog snappy for the rest of his life when people go to stroke him. Always insist on it being done in the soft part over the tummy in front of the hind leg. The dog, if held, won't even see it being done, and by the time he feels it the job is finished. Take special care that the puppy doesn't get chilled or come too much in contact with other dogs after he has received the inoculation; it takes time for a reasonable immunity to be built up.

EXERCISE

When your puppy has had his inoculations and is ready to go out into the outside world, you must decide on a routine of exercise to suit both you and your dog. A lot of nonsense is talked

All dogs enjoy a daily walk.

about exercising dogs. People spend hours in inclement weather braving the elements in order to give their puppies masses of exercise. As long as a puppy is allowed the freedom of the home, and is given one reasonable walk a day of about fifteen minutes, he will grow up perfectly all right. It is far more dangerous to over-exercise than under-exercise a puppy. This especially applies to large dogs like Wolfhounds and Great Danes and St Bernards. In fact, more puppies of these breeds have been spoilt by ignorant owners over-exercising them than by giving them too little exercise.

Ten minutes freedom in a field is worth half an hour's walk on the roads, for the puppy dashes about, backwards and forwards. With a smaller breed, such as a Scottish Terrier or a West Highland White Terrier, a puppy will be perfectly fit and well on half an hour's total exercise during the day. If you have time for more after he has reached the age of four months, by all means give him more, but for health purposes he doesn't need it, that is provided he gets the freedom of the home for part of the day.

It is far more dangerous to over-exercise than under-exercise a puppy, and this is particularly true in the fast-growing 'giant' breeds like St Bernards.

A small breed such as a West Highland White Terrier will keep fit and well on half an hour's total exercise a day.

GROOMING

Grooming is not absolutely necessary with a short-coated puppy that lives in the house, but the massaging effect that grooming has is beneficial to the skin; it helps circulation and removes dirt and dandruff. One need not have a stiff brush which might scratch your puppy; a baby's hairbrush is just as good. Finish off with an old piece of silk. When the puppy comes in from a muddy walk let him get dry and then brush the dried mud off. If you have an old towel dry him as much as possible with that and keep him very warm until quite dry. This is where a hair dryer comes in useful – a few minutes under that and the puppy is dry.

Long-haired puppies should have a brush and a comb in their toilet equipment, and the hair should always be brushed against the coat in the first place. This not only gets out tangles but it also stimulates the pores of the skin and removes any dead and broken hairs. Most puppies like being groomed. Any sign of temper must be firmly stopped. Right from the start, hold the puppy by a short lead on his choke chain, and if he snarls tighten the choke chain until he feels uncomfortable; loosen immediately he stops growling. Encourage the puppy with kind words all the time he is being groomed, and praise him a lot when you have finished. Your attitude towards this operation counts a lot, as does the gentle way you groom your puppy. One must realise that tangles hurt in dogs just as much as in humans. If the hair is very matted, damp it before attempting to get the tangles out. This helps enormously.

The best type of brush for any long-haired dog is the Mason Pearson type of wire-bristled brush. Nylon is not so good. It is a good idea to teach your puppy to lie on his side to be brushed. Always brush from his tummy left to right, and brush the hair towards you. After this, if you have brushed properly, you can comb the coat without pulling any hair out. Turn him on the other side and do the same thing. Should there be any matting of the coat, gently pull the matt apart with your finger and thumb, and then comb it through. Lastly stand him up and brush his topside. Always be sure to get the brush right down to the skin. Be very careful when brushing his head not to hurt his eyes by mistake. Always hold the ears in your hands and brush downwards and then upwards before combing. Short-haired dogs should be groomed with a hound-brush, which is worn over the owner's hand with the end of the thumb outside. This has the grooming part over the palm of the hand, and the puppy usually loves the massaging which this type of grooming gives him. Finish off with an old piece of silk to give a lovely bloom to the coat.

There is no hard and fast rule as to when a puppy changes his baby coat for a permanent adult one. It should begin at three months old and be fully in by eight months. It is essential to provide all the vitamins and minerals your puppy needs to develop a good coat. Also the temperature at which the puppy is kept makes a lot of difference. A good heavy coat is developed more quickly when a puppy is kept outside than when one is always in the warmth of the house. Be careful not to brush the puppy with too stiff a brush - you can make him bite by not being gentle

The amount of grooming a dog requires depends on the length and texture of coat. A smooth Fox Terrier is a low-maintenance breed.

enough. Until his permanent coat comes through a puppy hardly needs brushing, but it is a good idea to get him used to the grooming routine. Boiled linseed improves the texture of the coat and gives it a wonderful shine. Many show people feed their dogs with some boiled linseed before starting their show career. The linseed should be boiled in water until it forms a jelly when cold. A tablespoonful of the jelly a day is about right for a medium-sized puppy over six months old. I would not feed it to one any younger as it is inclined to make the puppy's bowels loose. The seeds of the linseed must, of course, be strained off, allowing only the liquid to come through the muslin you are straining it through.

Some puppies will have an undercoat and an over-length coat which is waterproof. German Shepherds have this double-texture coat. That is why they are suitable as shepherd dogs, as the weather does not affect them so

An Old English Sheepdog will require regular grooming, and a puppy should get used to this routine from an early stage.

much. Some puppies, like the Mexican Hairless, have no coat at all. Short-coated dogs are far easier to keep clean than long-coated ones, but they feel the cold much more. It is essential to keep a long-haired puppy's coat free from tangles. This especially applies to Old English Sheepdogs. Once the coat is really matted it is extremely difficult to comb it out. They should have a regular brushing and combing from an early age. This also applies to dogs like the Yorkshire Terrier. Puppies usually moult twice a year, with the exception of some breeds such as Poodles and West Highland White Terriers, which do not moult. When your puppy is moulting you should brush it at least once a day with a wire brush to get all the loose hairs out. A bath often works. Some people clip their Collies in summer as they get such heavy coats. That is, of course, if it is only a pet dog and not wanted for show.

Some owners like to put their dog in a coat in the winter. Obviously this comes down to a matter of personal choice. If the weather is wet and the puppy very young he should not be out for longer than is necessary for him to fulfil his toilet functions. But if you have to take him for a walk in inclement weather, a waterproof coat is a great asset. Very tiny puppies should not go for walks anyway. Puppies with long, natural coats are best protected from the wet, but do not feel the cold so much. You just have to use your common sense when it comes to putting a coat on your dog. Dogs should grow up reasonably hardy. On the other hand, most diseases start off with a bad chill, which allows the germs to get hold of the body. If chilling can be avoided by

the wearing of a coat, by all means put one on the puppy. One can now buy waterproof bootees for all-sized dogs, as well as waterproof coats and hats for Poodles. So if you really want to keep your puppy warm and dry, you can do so in all weathers!

BATHING

There is nothing injurious in the bathing process, and it may be necessary if your puppy smells or he has fleas. Fleas can be picked up time and time again from fields inhabited by chickens and other animals. Dogs infect one another, so a constant watch must be kept. Use a good dog soap – there are many available – to ensure there is no reinfestation of fleas, and be sure to disinfect the puppy's bedding at the same time.

No puppy suffers from having a bath, the trouble lies in getting him absolutely dry afterwards. Nowadays many people have home hair dryers. There is nothing better than a hair-dryer for drying a puppy. It not only dries him but gets him used to something new, which is always good. Be sure to keep your own hand underneath all the time to make sure he is not getting too hot. It must not be held too near the pup's tender skin. A good rub with rough towel to get the worst of the water off before using the hair dryer is always necessary.

NAIL CLIPPING

The cutting of a puppy's nails is really an expert's job. The breeder usually cuts them short before selling you the puppy, but if they are long take him along to a parlour where they strip dogs, or to the vet. Both should be able to do it and show you what to do. Exercising a puppy on the pavements should keep the nails down, it is only if the puppy never gets this road-work that they need cutting. In this instance the nails may need cutting every three weeks or so. It is best done with proper nail-clippers. Cut only the curved over piece that protrudes beyond the thick part which contains the quick. If you look at the nail from underneath it you will see that the end is almost transparent. That is the part to trim off. The paw should be held firmly and the nail cut straight across. You can then file the roughened tips with an emery board file. Always cut the nail to one sixth of an inch at the end of the quick – this allows sufficient protection. If by any chance you do cut the quick, wrap the whole nail up in a piece of plaster, it will soon grow out again. Some puppies are very frightened when you attempt to manicure them, and you will have to have help. Never give in to a puppy because he is reluctant to submit to the treatment. Bathing, manicuring and grooming are three things a puppy just has to learn.

TEETH

A puppy is born with no teeth; between two and three weeks he gets his milk teeth, which are very sharp, and he does not begin to lose these teeth until he is between three and five months old. At six months the permanent set of teeth should be complete. The changing of the teeth begins with the upper and lower incisors. It is amazing how quickly and unobtrusively a puppy loses its baby teeth and gains its permanent ones. Some people say they have seen baby

teeth all over the place, but this has not been my experience. Occasionally a permanent tooth will come down before the baby tooth has fallen out. If it is loose, you may be able to give the baby tooth a little tug, and it will come away easily. Otherwise, get your vet to pull the tooth out for you.

It is most important to examine a puppy's mouth quite often while teething to make sure nothing like an abscess is forming, or food becoming impacted where the baby tooth has fallen out. This examining of the mouth at frequent intervals is not only a safeguard against teething troubles, but a first-class way of accustoming the dog to having his mouth examined at shows later on, or for giving medicines, and for cleaning teeth at intervals. Frequent handling of a puppy's mouth makes him 'soft-mouthed' so that he won't nip so hard when playing with his owner. Baby teeth can do a lot of damage to the owner's fingers and arms – even though the puppy is only in play.

As the dog grows old the teeth deteriorate and become discoloured if not properly cleaned and scaled. This cleaning and scaling should be done regularly throughout the dog's life. Your vet or dog beauty parlour will do it for you. Few private owners are capable of carrying it out at home. The gums should be watched to ensure there is no overgrowth of gum caused by tartar on the teeth. If this does occur your vet will have to anaesthetise the dog and cut the gum back. This does not occur in puppies, only in older dogs. The age your puppy should first have its teeth cleaned cannot be forecast. Probably few puppies need this service until over the puppy stages. Bones help to clean the teeth and keep the gums healthy and free from pyorrhoea, But the bones should be large marrow bones, not game bones or small bones of any sort.

WORMING

Every puppy is born with a roundworm infestation, but luckily their days are numbered as soon as you dose your puppy with a suitable worm cure. The breeder will have wormed the litter, and you will need to repeat the treatment after the puppy has settled into his new home. There are a variety of products available on the market, and the puppy's breeder, or your vet can recommend a suitable one. Nowadays there is no need to starve a puppy before worming – simply pop the pill into his food. After about two hours the puppy will pass a motion with an abundance of dead worms. Should the puppy fail to clear after one dosing, he must be done again in a fortnight. Do not allow worm-infested puppies to lick children, or adults for that matter. The eggs are carried on the mouth of the puppy, and can be transmitted to man.

NURSING

Everyone hopes that their new puppy will be fit and healthy, but it is a good idea to have some knowledge about nursing a sick puppy, so you are prepared for all situations. Nursing a sick puppy is very like nursing a sick child. The conditions in most homes can be adapted so that the sick puppy has what he most needs, i.e. warmth, cleanliness, peace and quiet, plenty of clean water, and strict attention to diet,

and giving the medicines as prescribed by the vet in attendance. If you have more than one dog in the home, the sick one should be strictly isolated until all risk of passing on of infection has passed. The food should be as advised by the vet. The dishes the sick puppy eats from should be kept spotlessly clean. The utensils that that are used should be boiled once a day. The person looking after the sick puppy should be most careful to wash their hands after attending to the puppy. If possible, keep an overall or something old you can wear when seeing to the puppy. If the puppy is an only one in the house things are not so difficult. A lot of owners are so terribly worried over the puppy's illness that they keep rushing in to see how he is. This is bad for any sick animal. The puppy needs to sleep and conserve his energy. If you have an indoor kennel for him, that is where he should be. The kennel should be in a warm place right out of draughts, etc.

Another thing inexperienced people tend to do is to tempt the puppy all day long with food when he doesn't want it – they imagine he will die of starvation otherwise. An ill dog is best left without solid food for a couple of days; a light diet of milk and perhaps porridge is best. As he recovers he can be offered scraped meat in small quantities. It is most unwise to listen to well-meaning friends as to the cures they gave their dogs with the same symptoms; so many diseases have similar symptoms but are treated differently. Eggs, for example, would be unsafe for dogs with jaundice, only the whites should be given, yet in other diseases an egg is probably the most digestible food.

Try not to handle a sick puppy too much; naturally your love for him must be shown, but picking him up will tire him. Should he be frightened of the vet your assurance is very necessary. It is funny how so many dogs are frightened of the vet, yet he has never hurt them. I suppose it is the smell of antiseptics he carries about with him. A sick puppy should be able to lie stretched out in rest. Make sure his basket or kennel is big enough to allow this. Dogs pick up fear very easily, and I have known sensitive ones become worse when the owner has been terribly worried about them. Try and be cheerful when dealing with sick puppies, it gives them reassurance. I am perfectly certain animals worry over themselves if the owner worries. Remember you can often carry germs on your clothes, and therefore never handle anyone else's dog if you have a sick puppy at home.

One of the most difficult things to arrange is for a puppy to go outside to perform his toilet in winter, yet a house-trained puppy won't do it indoors. You must somehow fix up somewhere with a wind break for him, and be sure to put a coat on him before taking him out. Should he have diarrhoea, newspapers are the best thing to use in a kennel, they can be burnt. Remember, carbolic is death to dogs, so never disinfect anything with that. The puppy might chew something that has been washed in carbolic. Milton is absolutely safe, for even babies' bottles are washed in it.

Always be punctual in giving medicines. If a dose is once every four hours it should be given dead on time. One cannot gad around, coming home late, and still nurse a sick puppy. Always take away any food that the puppy refuses to eat, and throw it away; fresh food each meal-time is most important. Liver is the most tempting dish for a sick puppy; they adore it. But it gives a puppy diarrhoea if given in too great a quantity. If a puppy has pneumonia, a pneumonia jacket should be made for him out of surgical wadding. He should wear this for the whole duration of the pneumonia.

Occasionally when some ointment has to be applied to some irritating skin infection the puppy may have to be muzzled to prevent him eating it. Don't fret yourself that the muzzle is cruel; a well-fitting one hasn't the slightest bad effect on the puppy after the first shock of it is over. The main thing to remember is that you are doing everything you can to cure your puppy. He must not be handicapped in any way by over-sentimentality.

Chapter Six

FIRST STEPS IN TRAINING

'How soon shall I start training my puppy?' is a constant request that I get by letter. I think, contrary to some trainers' ideas, that a puppy is never too young, once he is weaned, to begin understanding small things. I put a very light cat's collar on a very small puppy so that he gets accustomed to wearing something round his neck. He will most likely sit down and scratch vigorously at first, and devote most of the first day to efforts to get rid of it, but harden your heart and pay no attention. If the puppy learns early that he must wear a collar there will be none of that fighting against it later on. Usually the owner gives up in despair and puts on dog braces. One cannot obedience-train a dog on braces, so that is a step backwards. If a dog arrives at my classes with braces I put on a choke chain collar and don't listen at all to the owner's assurance that: 'He won't wear a collar'. I don't believe that a dog in good hands should be allowed to have a say in what he will or won't do. The owner must be the judge in every case. If the owner is a fair-minded dog lover he will do nothing that is not right for

the dog, unless he does so from ignorance. And there is absolutely no excuse for ignorance on dog management in these days.

Very well then. We have bought an extremely light collar and the puppy has got used to wearing it. What about a lead? A very young puppy should definitely not be taken for walks in the accepted sense of the word. There is a grave risk of infection in the streets, and the puppy gets easily tired; but from about three months old he should have a lead on and be walked about for a short time each day. He is never too young to know that he must come back to your side on the command "Heel!" But serious training in this heelwork should not commence until the puppy is about three and a half months old. I don't think it matters what type of lead you have, as long as it isn't a chain one. This would cut your hand when carrying out the exercises. In my school I use a half-inch bridle leather leads, four feet long, with a safety Trojan hook. This type cannot open up with jerking, as can a scissor type. The ordinary spring hooks can come off the lead when

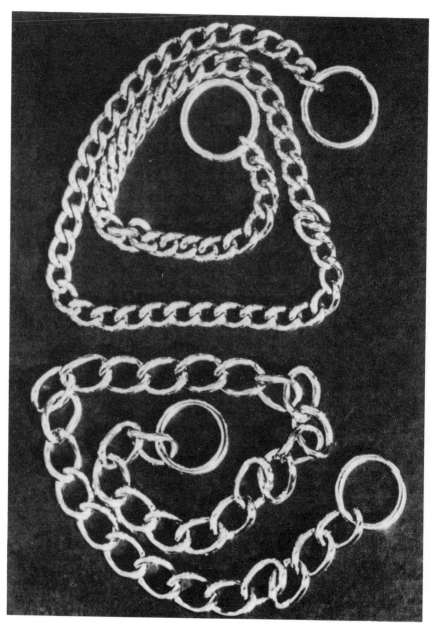

Choke chains: The broader the link, the kinder to the dog.

jerked and cut your hand. The lead should be held in the right hand when a puppy is being trained on your left hand side, and it must be held losely. Any tightness on a lead causes a dog to pull. Leather leads that get wet should be rubbed over with saddle soap and then polished with a soft rag. This preserves the leather. The hooks should have oil in the spring parts at least once a month. Never hold the lead over your wrist by the loop. If you happen to fall over you might get dragged by the dog.

It is most important not to allow the puppy to play with or chew his lead. This is an extremely bad habit which is very difficult to break. I had a dog arrive at my class one night that provides a good example of the folly of allowing the lead to become a plaything. Every time his master pulled on the lead, he stood up on his hindlegs and gripped the lead in a vice-like grip with his front paws. That meant one could not pull the lead at all to any good purpose. The only way to break this habit was to pull the dog sharply to the ground whenever he did it. If a puppy learns while walking to play with the lead he never recognises its authority and just bites it when you wish to give him a jerk.

A puppy should be taught from the age of twelve weeks to wear a thick-linked choke chain. They range in size from twelve inches up to twenty-six inches, although you can have any size made to order. The way to measure the length you need is to take a piece of string or tape and measure round the dog's chin and up over his ears, then allow two inches extra for getting it over the head and for growth. The chain should always have two or three links hanging free on the pulling end of the choke chain. The thin-linked variety are not so kind, and as you have to snatch hard at the lead to correct a pulling puppy, you do need the thick links to prevent any bruising. There is no pain in using a choke chain, only breathlessness, if not released quickly enough. The chain should never be tight; the dog should be jerked back and instantly loosed. If the jerk and simultaneous command are sharp enough, then the puppy will learn in a few minutes. Anyone who says choke chains are cruel, when used correctly, is ignorant. They are only used to prevent injury to ears and neck from the use of a leather collar. Leather collars that run with a ring on them are useless for training, and so are braces. I think it is high time the term 'choke chain' was changed to 'check chain'. It is to check the dog kindly. It is only used to choke him temporarily if he bites or is fighting.

The puppy is never too young to be taught that when you say "Bed" or "Box" or "Basket" or the name of whatever else you may have as a home for him, you mean that puppy to go to his bed and stay there until you want him. If he gets up to go away, he must be firmly put back with the command "Stay in your bed." Give him a gentle pat to soothe him before you go away. Naturally the puppy would rather be playing with you or dashing about than staying in his basket, but this training is so very important. All his life there will be times when he must stay quietly in a certain place when you can't have him with you, and it is his early training that matters. If he barks or howls, go back to him and scold him. Never think 'Poor little puppy, I'll take him on my lap.' If you do, you've lost the first battle. But

To use: (1) Hold by both rings. (2) Drop chain through one ring. (3) Put on dog pulling upwards. (4) The chain automatically loosens when used correctly.

Correct: The proper way to use a choke chain.

Wrong: A chain incorrectly put on a dog.

on the other hand, never leave a puppy too long. Once he has obeyed and stayed quietly in the box for some time, try, if you can manage it, to give him a romp. I cannot impress on my readers too strongly the necessity to be firm but kind to a puppy. His idea of your authority is forming, and if he knows you give in on the slightest whimper, you are whacked for life. To break him of habits formed when young is far more tiresome than training him in the right way at first.

Barking is an inexcusable trick, and if the puppy continues to do it, make sure he is not wanting to go out, make sure he is comfortable and warm, and not hungry. If you are certain on all these points, leave him to yell, only coming back at intervals to speak to him firmly.

Then settle him down again quietly and with gentle stroking and words of encouragement, leave him again. Under no circumstances take the dog out of his box when he is yelling, except to make certain all is well. If the puppy thinks he is going to be picked up or let out, you are lost. Usually a puppy will cry for two or three nights at first, on leaving his old home; he misses the warmth and comfort of the rest of the litter or his mother, and his box is a frightening thing to be left alone in. But harden your heart and just try not to listen. Warmth is the all-powerful cure for this sort of thing at night. No puppy can help becoming sleepy in a really warm bed.

The next thing we must stop is the impulse to chew up every thing he sees.

This is, of course, a natural thing to do; he is cutting his teeth and he wants to gnaw everything in sight to help his troublesome little teeth through. The answer is, of course, to give him plenty of material that he is allowed to chew. My puppies always have bones in plenty, big marrow bones, not tiny ones that might splinter. A rubber bone is useful, or a hard old dog biscuit, or even an old slipper. Give the puppy plenty to play with, but as soon as he touches something that he must not, the firm command and the words "No, naughty!" must come in. Take the object away and then offer it to him again; if he goes to take it, scold him severely and give the command "Leave!" Offer it again, and repeat the word "Leave!" He will soon know that he must not touch that article.

The same applies to food stealing. If you can catch him stealing, take the food away and scold him with the same "Leave!" command. Offer it again, and so on. When you give him his own dinner, give it to him with a lot of praise and always in his own dish. If you use several different plates it is difficult for the dog to know what he may and what he may not take. Teach him to have a piece of meat put between his feet with the command "Leave!" and then a second or two later pick it up and give it to him with much praise. Anything you give him is right, anything he just takes is wrong. That will help when people offer him things to eat in the street: he will await your permission before taking it. Do keep to very regular meal times for your puppy. My dogs know the time to a second, and I make a point of feeding them (and, incidentally, all my animals) absolutely by the clock. If I

happen to be out driving I stop and feed the dog at the right time. I always take their food with me. It keeps their digestions happy, as nature has a peculiar way of making the saliva run and the digestive juices flow ready to digest the meal at those times. I have often seen my dog dribbling at the right time for a meal.

Jumping up is, in my opinion, one of the greatest curses of owning an untrained dog. With a puppy, one is inclined to forgive it as just a show of exuberance, but later on, when the dog comes in with muddy paws and jumps up for play, or a kiss, it can be the ruination of a dress or suit. Therefore stop this trick in the beginning. I always kneel down when really praising a small dog, so that the inclination to jump up needn't arise. The dog only jumps up to be near your face. Faces have a fascination for dogs. A well-trained dog never takes his eyes off his master while working in a competition, and this eagerness to be near his master's face begins very early in life. However, if your puppy persists in jumping up, firmer measures may be needed. The puppy must be taught to wait on command by putting him on a long string and tying it to something strong. Put your dog in the sit so that the string is completely loose and call him. before he has time to reach you, give the command "wait" and hold up your hand, all fingers outstretched. If he doesn't stop, give him the command again when he is nearing the end of the string, the string will stop him, when you must then go and scold him. Repeat until he stops in his tracks on the command "wait", and then praise him. This training will only work if you

An untrained dog that jumps up at everyone can be a curse to own.

have taught your puppy to come; titbits are permissible. If he won't come you must use the string again, to pull him into you this time. Give him some sharp jerks towards you, coinciding with the word "come"; he will find it unpleasant not to come. Now when he dashes about your house, stop him with the word 'wait', and you can then put him away where he can do no damage. This will soon teach him to behave. Jumping up must be stopped by a sharp slap on the nose as he jumps up. There is no other way, except by hitting his nose with a wet rag. But how often does one have a wet rag in one's hand at that particular moment? Dogs hate being hit with a wet rag; it has a most sobering effect on them.

Quite often I am asked: 'Am I likely to catch any disease if I kiss my dog?' I always reply that only one ill is communicable to man from dogs and that is the tapeworm, so if you want to kiss your dog don't kiss his nose or muzzle. I always lay my face against a dog's cheek so that I can whisper sweet nothings into his ear. I have trained our little English Toy Terrier to wait for a kiss; she puts her head on one side and waits until I give her a kiss before showing terrific pleasure by really lifting up her upper lip in a toothy smile. Sometimes I have to give her five or six kisses before she is satisfied: I really have to love her a lot! Dogs adore affection. I know very few owners who really give their dogs all the affection they need. Of course there are cranks who overdo it, but we are not concerned with such people, who probably lack love in their normal human relations and who therefore give exaggerated affection to their dogs and

expect it to be returned. One must have a reasonable perspective in these matters.

I know a dog caresses by licking; it is his way of showing love and appreciation of the person he does it to. But if he is stopped doing this as a small puppy, he still learns to lay his face against the owner's cheek without the licking. Licking, after all, can be a cause of infection to owners in rare cases and not all dogs live a completely clean life. They eat manure, or lick their behinds – not only their own but those of other dogs who might not be so healthy as yours. Therefore I trained all my dogs on the command "No lick" to be kissed by me behind their ears and to have their chests very slowly and gently scratched. Excessive licking by dogs of their bodies may mean allergic reaction, may mean too full anal glands, or it may mean a skin disease. People sometimes imagine dogs wash themselves like cats; well, they don't do this like cats. Sometimes when they get their paws wet, you will see dogs licking them to dry them as does a bitch lick her puppies to dry and clean them. Dogs should be allowed to lick one's hand; one can easily wash one's hands before touching food, but generally licking should be avoided and stopped at an early age.

I believe it is essential to talk to your dog as frequently as you would to a child. You will be amazed how much your dog understands, not only by the tone of your voice but from actual words. I save myself many an unnecessary journey by asking my dog to go and 'shut the door' or 'fetch the newspaper', etc. I have no trouble at all in teaching her a new thing to do,

A dog can be caressed without the need for licking.

because she knows so many basic words, as for example, 'go', 'fetch', 'bring', 'put it over there', 'come', 'sit', 'stay', 'down', 'away', 'corner', 'go round', 'turn round', 'walk back', etc.; in fact, there are a vast number of combinations of words in a dog's dictionary. It is your business to help him build up this vocabulary, beginning with his name, then simple words like 'Box!' 'Leave!' and 'Naughty!' already mentioned, then perhaps 'Bone', 'Dinner', and the various names of objects or actions that fill him with pleasure or excitement. As his comprehension of single words grows, so does his power of understanding separate sounds strung together.

No one knows why touch is so important. I think probably blind people know more than any of us about the sensitivity of touch; that is why guide dogs are usually so faithful. But the ordinary handler can develop this touch which calms the wild dog, which produces ecstasy in dogs when you caress them, but it has to come through the fingers or face direct from your heart. In every training school the words: 'Praise your dog' are heard constantly; by those words in my school I don't necessarily mean a big hearty pat. I mean a communion of brain and touch. I lay my face alongside that of the dog with its face cupped in my hands, and I sense that my deep love and admiration for it passes right through to its mind, often in silent communion, for I have already said "What a good dog" and clapped my hands to show approval at the end of the exercise. Praise can be given in so many ways, by titbits for a puppy, by tone of voice, by scratching a dog's chest, by firm warm pats on the back, by kissing, which all dogs love, or by just looking straight into their eyes and smiling. You can't deceive dogs. It doesn't matter whether you say "Good dog" or "Gadzooks". The dog knows what you mean.

We come now to the vexed question of how much encouragement a puppy should get to bark at the telephone or at the doorbell, of how to teach him to stop barking or start barking. It is quite easy to teach him to bark by getting someone to bang on the door,

whereupon you rush towards it with tremendous excitement, 'barking' yourself and getting terrifically worked up. The dog soon understands this game and should learn under an hour what he is supposed to do. The greater trouble comes when you want to stop him. As he barks, you go to the door and open it. If it is a friend, you tell the dog "That will do" and if he doesn't stop barking immediately, scold him and straightaway put him, lying down, into his kennel. He will soon come to connect the words 'That will do' with being put in his kennel, or down, and as you say "That will do" he will soon learn to stop barking in anticipation of being put in his box. He also connects the words with a scolding. But always remember to praise him, when he barks at first with "Good boy!" then follow it by "That will do" and the command to go and lie down. Few dogs bark much when lying down.

Some dogs bark for hours if left alone in the house. The reason for this is loneliness, and the barking is really a compliment to the owner. But it is also a vice, and must be stopped. The only way to stop it is to train your dog while you are in the house to be put in another room with its blanket or basket, and to stay there quietly. At first it will bark very loudly. The owner must return very crossly and send him to his basket with extremely angry words. The dog will try to fawn over the owner, but under no circumstances must one give in. When you have got him lying down, change your tone of voice to a soft soothing one, and with plenty of praise tell him to "Stay, there's a good boy," leaving him in a slow, comforting manner. If the dog is quiet for about half an hour go back and praise him with all the fervour you can muster, let him romp about, and take him with you to your sitting room or wherever you are; show him that you think he is the cleverest and most wonderful dog you know. If you do this daily your dog will learn that you are coming back and will eventually lie down quietly wherever you put him. But this is not taught in a day, and is never taught at all by a weak-willed owner. I maintain that to train a dog successfully the owner must be absolutely determined that with kindness and firmness he will make the dog do as it is told. The dog must get the impression that if he doesn't do right there is going to be real trouble with him, but if he does do right he's going to have a wonderful time.

I think you will find that a dog that has been trained to stay anywhere quietly in a house will also stay happily in the street in your car. I often think a dog is best left in a car rather than outside a shop, although I am often shocked by the way owners shut the windows up tight in hot weather until the dog is really suffering. One's dog should be so trained that if the windows are all open a few inches he will not try to get out. At first, give him his own blanket or cushion on the back seat, so that he has the comfort of familiar things around him. He should bark if a stranger comes too close to the car he is guarding. It is natural for any dog to guard his owner's property.

If you want your puppy to be really intelligent, you must, as far as possible, take him with you wherever you go. Rides in the car should be a pleasure, not a curse. If you have a hatchback, you will have no trouble with your dog as you can put up a dog-guard or some wire netting to separate him from the passenger seats, and he will not annoy anyone. If you want to train your puppy to go on the back seat, this can best be achieved by tying a rope to the puppy's collar and attaching it to some part of the car, so that the puppy can move about, but he cannot get off the seat. By far the best thing is to teach him to sit or stay in the back. You will need a helper to do this, because at first, the dog will get up again and again. Only by being firm and pushing him down as often as he gets up, with a firm command "down", can you hope to teach this lesson. Obviously this cannot be done at the same time as driving. If the puppy is not too big he can have a kennel made like a rabbit hutch, and put on the back seat. Thus, the puppy can see out, but he cannot get out. he will soon get used to being in there alone, and can later be free. Fold-up wire kennels are excellent. Everything to do with puppies is learnt by force of habit. Once you have accustomed a puppy to doing something at a certain time or in a certain manner, he will continue to do it in the future, without a fuss. Some puppies suffer from car-sickness or 'slobber' all over their owner when in the car. This type of car sickness is caused by lack of trust. If you take your puppy with you everywhere, from his earliest days, he will soon get used to the car's motion. The puppy should lie on someone's lap to begin with, and not on the car floor. Tie a bib round the dog's neck if necessary, and make sure he has had no food before a journey. With obedience training, car sickness disappears. It is only highly strung puppies who suffer from this trouble.

placid puppies are not car sick. If the owner is perpetually worrying about the puppy, the puppy will be sick. Put some old blankets in the car, and do not worry, provided the puppy has not been fed, he will only dribble saliva which easily sponges off.

A trained dog is one that trusts his owner and the outside world. He is usually calm under all circumstances, is seldom car sick, is seldom a fighter, and takes in his stride any upheaval in the home. This trust only comes with daily training, with firm insistence on immediate obedience and then much praise. I think most of the mental upsets, except schizophrenia, are caused by owners. I think most puppies are born normal, but some are made abnormal by their upbringing. Too

many people are over-sentimental and lack clear, firm commands. They end up with dirty dogs, biting dogs, disobedient dogs for several reasons. They think the dogs will grow out of their faults; this seldom happens. They think biting puppies are only biting because they are teething; this is wrong. Puppies bite because they want to be master. In sensible circles we don't allow puppies to teethe or bite on our fingers; a firm command "No bite" puts an end to this. One other reason for lack of correction is the owner's words 'Oh, he's so sweet'. Sweet the puppy may be at ten weeks, but he may turn out to be a likely candidate for being put to sleep at twelve months if he is allowed to continue unchecked.

Chapter Seven

UNDERSTANDING YOUR PUPPY

In the dog's mind, a master or a mistress to love, honour and obey is an absolute necessity. The love is dormant in the dog until brought into full bloom by an understanding owner. Thousands of dogs appear to love their owners, they welcome them home with enthusiastic wagging of the tail and jumping up, they follow them about their houses happily and, to the normal person seeing the dog, the affection is true and deep. But to the experienced dog trainer this outward show is not enough. The true test of real love is when the dog has got the opportunity to go out on his own as soon as a door is left open by mistake, and he goes off and often doesn't return for hours. That dog only loves his home comforts and the attention he gets from his family; he doesn't truly love the master or mistress, as they fondly think. True love in dogs only comes when every door can be open and the dog will still stay happily within earshot of his owner. For the owner must be the be-all and end-all of a dog's life. To achieve this the owner has to master the dog at some time or other as the leader of the pack

did in bygone days. There must be no question as to who is the boss of the house; it must be the owner. Dogs not only love owners who have had at one time a battle of wills for supremacy, they adore them, for a dog is really a subservient creature by nature, longing to trust his true love to someone's heart.

Now we come to the word 'honour', or, as I prefer it, 'respect.' This respect in a dog's mind is paramount, and I can't repeat often enough that, without respect which includes a certain amount of 'righteous fear' as the Bible would say, the dog lacks something in his essential make-up which sentimentality cannot replace. When I use the words 'righteous fear' women in particular shrink with horror; they wouldn't like their dogs to be frightened of them. When I explain that righteous fear is not being frightened, they don't understand. The reason humans don't all steal, lie or what have you, is simply because in most of us there is a righteous fear of the results. In dogs it should be the same. If they run off or fight another dog, their minds must be educated to know that there will be a reprisal and,

The owner must be the be all and end all in the dog's life.

without this righteous fear, the dog will never be completely happy, for dogs love looking up to their owners or, as the case may be, their trainers.

It is indeed very sad for me to see the number of dogs whose minds are forever tuned-in to mine in a class when they should be tuned-in to their owners' thoughts and wishes. The reason is, I make them immediately do as I wish, and then give abundant praise. Many owners, in a distorted sense of kindness, let the dogs get away with disobedience, or make them do it so slowly that there is no respect for the owner from the dog. In fact many dogs show this in no mean way by biting their owners. When a dog bites his owner I feel sure it is mostly done as a last desperate resort to rouse the owner into being someone the dog can respect. Once the owner has got that respect the dog can be taught everything with the least possible number of scoldings or corrections. A dog loves to learn things and adores to please. Once the hurdle of respect has been jumped, the continuation of training goes smoothly.

This sequence of events is very hard to teach the owners, for a vast number of dog owners have no idea what their dog prefers. They think dogs adore sentimentality. Dogs do up to a certain point, but even the tiniest of toy dogs wants a proper owner to love and respect; just because he only weighs 2lb doesn't mean he has no character or that he should not be obedient. People are now finding out that the tiniest Yorkshire Terrier, for example, has a brain big enough to do first class obedience; his mind works the same as a Great Dane's mind; he also wants to respect his owner. There is no difference between men owners and women owners as regards over-sentimentality. In fact, I have found some men to be more stupidly sentimental than women and when I have to be firm with their dogs they feel very badly about it. Yet the dogs show which they prefer and every time it is the strong-minded but loving handler who gets real love and implicit obedience from the dog.

If a dog is cringing and frightened I always know the owner has not been firm enough, for this type of dog needs someone to respect more than any other; he is weak-natured and likes to draw courage and strength from a firm owner. What do I mean by the word 'firm'? I use it so often that people may think I mean, 'Get a stick and beat the dog.' This is far from my mind. In fact, I think owners should practically never smack a dog, for it is a sign of defeat on the owner's part. It means that the dog's progressive training and the development of his mind and intelligence has not been accomplished. It means the owner has to resort to something that may be beyond his own strength. It is degrading for both dog and owner, for a dog that has been firmly but kindly trained never needs a beating. No, firmness in my estimation means a firmness of purpose, a strength of will that doesn't take defeat however long it takes to succeed. A firmness that is gentle as well as strong, for, make no mistake, a disobedient and wilful dog needs prolonged patience and perseverance to win.

By being firm I mean setting the dog something to do and making him do it, knowing in your own mind that that which you wish him to do is fair and

A dog responds to firm, decisive commands.

right and necessary for his and your happy co-existence. He may fight, scream as if being murdered, or just bite you in retaliation, or may just seem mortally afraid; all these ruses can be tried on by a dog when asked to obey. If you are not firm your inner heart revolts at making him obey, and you are sorry for his whimperings or his apparent fear or defiance. You let up and let him get his own way. The seeds of disrespect are sown and will accordingly germinate, to the ultimate misery of both owner and dog. Often in my class I meet these disrespectful dogs who don't truly love their owners. But the owners are mightily annoyed when I tell them their dogs don't really love them. They assure me the dog never leaves them in the house, etc; but it cuts no ice with me. I know that once I have shown the owners how much their dogs prefer me to them after I have made them carry out my wishes, they will be converted. I think the old motto, 'You have to be cruel to be kind,' should be changed for dog owners to, 'You have to be firm to be kind.' Firmness only has to be continued until the right kind of respect enters the dog's mind. And, when being firm, unending praise and affection must be given to the dog.

This praise and affection is where a multitude of owners fail their dogs. A pat and a kind word are not enough in the initial training of dogs; the atmosphere must be charged with a certain excitement, for dogs are very sensitive to excitement; when they have done right, they love having the wildest show of affection and a good romp round. Dull owners make dull dogs, stony-faced owners, zip-lipped owners, and inhibited owners tend to have dull,

disobedient dogs, who take a long time to learn obedience. The dog's mind is only equal to a child's mind and, as comedy makes up a big part of a child's life, it should do the same in a dog's life. Dogs love laughter, clapping and jokes. I had a little dog who laughed when we laughed, although she hadn't the slightest idea what she was laughing about. It was the happiness that pervaded the room when we were laughing that entered her brain and made her feel happy, so she smiled too. Try smiling at everyone you meet down the street; you will be amazed how many complete strangers smile back before they zip up again, realising they don't know you. It is the same with dogs even if they don't know you; they respond to a smile and a clap if they have done well. They watch your eyes and face for the happy sign that you are pleased. I am intensely sorry for the dogs who see no smiles on their owners' faces. You can't train a dog well if you are unhappy; your tenseness communicates itself to the dog, and the dog becomes depressed.

What a wonderful indicator of happiness is the dog's tail; the half-mast wag with the very tip of the tail, showing nervous expectation; the half-mast slow wag of the interested dog who wants to know what master is saying but doesn't quite pick it up; the full-mast wag of excitement and happiness when he is really happy; and, last but not least, the tail between the legs of the nervous, shy or unhappy dog who trusts no one and to whom life is a burden. When a dog is happily learning, or happily obeying I like to see its tail at the medium sensible height; when having a game after lessons or when

The dog's mind is equal to a child's mind, and like a child it loves laughter and jokes.

free I like the full mast. But what I like most is to change in a matter of minutes the tail between the legs to the half-mast by firm and sensible handling, for this can be done in minutes if you get through to the dog's mind and give strength to him by your own forceful happiness and strength of purpose. A dog that loves, honours and consequently obeys is a joy to himself and his owner.

APPENDIX

A range of other books, tapes and accessories are available to help you derive the full benefit from the Barbara Woodhouse approach to dog training.

Other titles in this series are:

Barbara Woodhouse On How Your Dog Thinks

Barbara looks at the world from the dog's viewpoint, and comes up with some new and surprising theories on dog behaviour. She shows owners how to understand their dogs and to communicate with them, not just by words and commands, but by tone of voice, and body language. In this book Barbara Woodhouse uses her rare gifts to break down the barriers, and helps all owners to achieve perfect companionship with their dogs.

Barbara Woodhouse On Training Your Dog

Barbara guides the owner through the first steps of basic obedience, essential for the family pet, and graduates, stage by stage, to more advanced and specialised training. This book is essential for every owner who wants their dog to be "a pleasure to all, and a nuisance to none."

Barbara Woodhouse On Handling A Problem Dog

Whether it is an aggressive dog, a nervous dog, a roaming dog or a thief, Barbara Woodhouse believes that with proper understanding, most faults can be cured quickly and a happy relationship can be built up between owner and dog. At this time, more than any other, it is essential that all dogs are well behaved and live in harmony with their owners and with society. Barbara, who has trained some 19,000 dogs, tackles a wide spectrum of 'problem dogs' and comes up with sound, commonsense solutions.

Barbara Woodhouse On Keeping Your Dog Healthy

In a lifetime spent boarding, breeding and training dogs, she has come across all the most common conditions and complaints affecting dogs, and she gives practical, no-nonsense advice on all aspects of dog care, from diet, exercise and grooming to breeding, diagnosing health problems and nursing a dog through a serious illness. When you buy a dog, you are responsible for all its physical and mental needs, and this book tells you all you need to know to be a firm, fair and loving owner.

All these titles should be available through your local pet or book shop, price £3.99 each. In cases of difficulty they can be ordered direct from the publisher. (Please add 75p per title towards P&P). See address at the end of this section.

The Complete Woodhouse Guide To Dog Training

This is the definitive volume on dog training from Britain's best-loved expert.
Everything you need to know about the care and control of your dog; how to understand his behaviour and how to get the best from him.
This book contains the very best of Barbara Woodhouse's writing on a subject she understands like no other.
Available from good bookshops everywhere, price £14.95

In case of difficulty The Complete Woodhouse Guide To Dog Training can be ordered direct from the publisher.
(Please add £1.50 towards P&P).
See address at the end of this section.

And if you've read the book, it is time to see the movie!

THE *WOODHOUSE* VIDEO
Barbara Woodhouse:
Quick Dog Training

A complete programme of obedience exercises for you and your dog. This 90 minute video takes you step-by-step through all the essential commands: Sit, Stay, Wait, Down, Leave and Recall.
PLUS house training, giving medicine, obedience in the car and on the street, walking to heel and much, much more from the most celebrated dog trainer in the world.

Price: £14.99
(plus £1.50 P&P)

Available ONLY from the publisher.
See address at the end of this section

BARBARA WOODHOUSE
CHOKE CHAINS AND LEADS
Are also available through the publisher

CHOKE CHAINS

Sizes at two–inch intervals
Twelve inches to eighteen inches   £3.00
Twenty inches to Twenty-eight inches   £3.50

To obtain the correct choke chain, measure over the top of the dog's head, down over the ears and under the chin, then add two inches and round up or down to the nearest size.
Please add 95p P&P to each order

LEADS

Approx four foot long in best quality bridle leather
Large or small trigger hooks   £5.95
Please add 95p P&P to each order

BARBARA WOODHOUSE AUDIO CASSETTE

BASED ON THE SERIES
TRAINING DOGS THE WOODHOUSE WAY
Price: £5.95
(including postage and packing)

HOW TO ORDER

All the items described here can be ordered
direct from the publisher

RINGPRESS BOOKS LTD.,
SPIRELLA HOUSE, BRIDGE ROAD,
LETCHWORTH, HERTS SG6 4ET

Please remember to add postage and packing charge where
necessary and allow 21 days for delivery.

ACCESS and VISA card holder may order by telephone on
0462 674177

Office open 9am to 5pm Monday to Friday